The Cherokee

Life Before the

edited by Madeleine Meyers

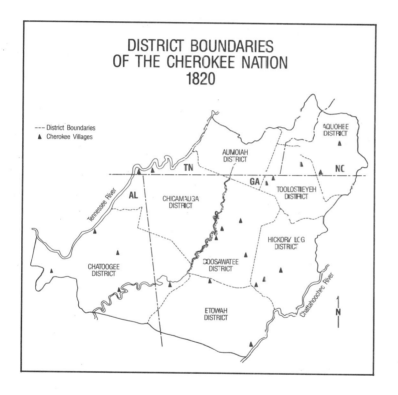

DISTRICT BOUNDARIES
OF THE CHEROKEE NATION
1820

--- District Boundaries
▲ Cherokee Villages

AQUOHEE
DISTRICT

AUMOIAH
DISTRICT

TN

GA

NC

Tennessee River

AL

CHICAMAUGA
DISTRICT

TOOLOSTIEYEH
DISTRICT

HICKORY LOG
DISTRICT

CHATOOGEE
DISTRICT

COOSAWATEE
DISTRICT

Chattahoochee River

ETOWAH
DISTRICT

N

© Discovery Enterprises, Ltd.
Lowell, Massachusetts
1994

© Discovery Enterprises, Ltd., Lowell, MA 1994

ISBN 1-878668-26-9 paperback edition
Library of Congress Catalog Card Number 93-70437

10   9   8   7   6   5   4   3   2   1

Printed in the United States of America

Subject Reference Guide:

Cherokee Indians – Juvenile nonfiction
North American Indian History – Southern States
Sequoyah – Biography – Juvenile nonfiction

Acknowledgments

I wish to express my appreciation to Dr. Thomas A. Scott of Kennesaw State College, Kennesaw, Georgia, and to Jeff Stancil of the New Echota State Historic Site, Calhoun, Georgia, for their assistance in researching this book.

I also wish to thank my parents, Rose and Richard C. Meyers, Jr., for being my eyes and legs in Georgia and North Carolina.

Table of Contents

Dedication

Dedicated to those people who are working so hard to keep the traditions of the Cherokee Indians alive.

Foreword

At the southern end of the Appalachians, in the soft green majesty of the Smoky Mountains is one of the largest Indian reservations in the Eastern part of the United States. It is the home of the Eastern Band of Cherokees who live in a small part of what was once the Cherokee Nation. Many are direct descendants of the Cherokees who hid from soldiers to avoid being taken away on the Trail of Tears. This modern band is involved in the crucial effort to keep alive the traditions of those earlier Cherokees who were forcefully removed from their land.

The Cherokee Indians were a handsome people of Iroquois descent who migrated to the area from the North. Before 1700, they had lived for a long time in a territory of approximately 40,000 square miles. Their lives centered around growing crops, hunting, and performing ritual ceremonies. They lived in settlements which contained bark-covered houses, a ceremonial ground, and a large seven-sided council building.

In William McLoughlin's book on the Cherokee renascence he tells us that their lives were structured by customs, rituals, beliefs, and ceremonies. Unity came from common customs and clan membership. There were seven clans, and every settlement had representatives from each of the clans. Each settlement was self-governing and allowed both men and women to speak at council meetings. Social order was kept by their belief in harmony in all parts of life. Children were taught from an early age that the needs of the community were very important, and that offenses like lying and stealing would be punished by the community. Shunning was one of the punishments they used.

The towns had communal gardens, where the women grew corn, beans, melons, squash, and tobacco. They also ate fish from ponds and rivers, and gathered wild berries and nuts. The men hunted with bows and arrows, traps, snares, and blowguns.

However, as the years passed and the Cherokees came into more frequent contact with White men, their lives began to change. As the Indians learned to hunt with guns, they had surplus game with which to trade for steel traps, knives, farming implements, and manufactured goods. This more efficient hunting method quickly depleted the local game, forcing the Cherokees to hunt farther and farther away. They also lost large tracts of their hunting grounds to White settlers through various treaties and agreements.

As the White man moved into the area, the Cherokees adopted many of their ways. In time, the women began using pots and pans instead of their ancient clay pottery. They purchased cloth and blankets, and learned to spin and weave. Gradually, the bark-covered houses gave way to log cabins, and the communal gardens turned into individual farms. They also began to raise cattle on their farms.

In 1789, George Washington outlined a plan to Congress to guide the U.S. relations with the American

Indians. Part of this policy was based on the "civilization" of Indians, describing how they would become citizens. As the Cherokees interacted with the White man they came to believe that this "civilization" was the only way to save their nation, so they worked very hard to become what the White man wanted.

At the beginning of the 1800s, a new group of leaders emerged and began to direct the Cherokee Nation. Many of them were the sons of intermarriages between the Cherokees and the White people. As they became more educated they attempted to conduct their business on an equal basis with the White man, negotiating in Washington and taking disputes to the U.S. court system.

The Cherokees organized themselves as a civil nation. They formed a bicameral legislature known as the General Council, which was composed of a National Council and a National Committee. The nation was divided into eight districts. Each district had a judge, marshal, and council. The districts also sent elected representatives to the General Council. In 1826 they held a constitutional convention in their capitol, New Echota. The resulting constitution was similar to that of the United States, with executive, judicial, and legislative branches. The head of their government was the Principal Chief. John Ross was elected to that post in 1828.

With the development of their own alphabet the Cherokees entered a more advanced phase. They began publishing a bilingual newspaper called "The Cherokee Phoenix." They also translated and printed over 700,000 pages of books and documents in the

John Ross

Cherokee language, and established book societies
to circulate these new materials.

During those years missionaries came to the
Cherokee Nation bringing both religion and schools.
Many Cherokee parents were willing to send their children to those schools, and, by the 1820s, there had
been a substantial growth in formal education. The
missionaries also supported the Cherokees' fight to

keep their lands. Two were even sent to jail for their efforts on behalf of the Indians.

Unfortunately, the Cherokees were forced off their lands, despite their own efforts and those of their supporters. In 1828, gold was discovered near present day Dahlonega, Georgia, sending thousands of prospectors into the Cherokee Nation. In December of 1829, President Andrew Jackson told the American Congress of his intention to move all Indians to the West. Congress passed the Indian Removal Bill in 1830.

Not even a decree by the U.S. Supreme Court in 1832, reaffirming that the Cherokee Nation was a "distinct community, occupying its own territory" over which other states had no jurisdiction, could save them. By the end of the decade, in a sad chapter of United States history called the Trail of Tears, the Cherokees were removed from their lands to make way for the ever-increasing number of settlers who would eventually occupy the country from ocean to ocean.

The political and historical events leading up to the Trail of Tears have been chronicled in many books. In this book, however, you will find information about the lives of the original Indians, their myths, and some information about their "civilized" period. The primary source materials, myths, and poetry in this book give you a glimpse of Cherokee life, before the tears.

— Madeleine Meyers

Legends

In every culture, myths and legends are passed along orally from generation to generation. They sometimes explain the otherwise unexplainable, and they often record historic events. The three legends here tell the story of the beginning of man on earth.

In the late 1800s, James Mooney travelled extensively among the Cherokee people, interviewing them and recording their history and social customs. He learned the secret formulas of their shamans (medicine men) and many of their legends, or myths as he called them. Here are three of the many myths that Mooney published.

How The World Was Made

The earth is a great island floating in a sea of water, and suspended at each of the four cardinal points by a cord hanging down from the sky vault, which is of solid rock. When the world grows old and worn out, the people will die and the cords will break and let the earth sink down into the ocean, and all will be water again. The Indians are afraid of this.

When all was water, the animals were above in Galun'-lati, beyond the arch; but it was very much crowded, and they were wanting more room. They wondered what was below the water, and at last Dayuni'si, "Beaver's Grandchild," the little Water-beetle, offered to go and see if it could learn. It darted in every direction over the surface of the water, but could find no firm place to rest. Then it dived to the bottom and came up with some soft mud, which began to grow and spread on every side until it became the island which we call the earth. It was afterward fastened to the sky with four cords, but no one remembers who did this.

At first the earth was flat and very soft and wet. The animals were anxious to get down, and sent out different birds to see if it was yet dry, but they found no place to alight and came back again to Galun'lati. At last it seemed to be time, and they sent out the Buzzard and told him to go and make ready for them. This was the Great Buzzard, the father of all the buzzards we see now. He flew all over the earth, low down near the ground, and it was still soft. When he reached the Cherokee country, he was very tired, and his wings began to flap and strike the ground, and wherever they struck the earth there was a valley, and where they turned up again there was a mountain. When the animals above saw this, they were afraid that the whole world would be mountains, so they called him back. but the Cherokee country remains full of mountains to this day.

When the earth was dry and the animals came down, it was still dark, so they got the sun and set it in a track to go every day across the island from east to west, just overhead. It was too hot this way, and Tsiska'gili', the Red Crawfish, had his shell scorched a bright red, so that his meat was spoiled; and the Cherokee do not eat it. The conjurers put the sun another hand-breadth higher in the air, but it was still too hot. They raised it another time, and another, until it was seven hand-breadths high and just under the sky arch. Then it was right, and they left it so. This is why the conjurers call the highest place Gulkwa'gine Di'galun'-latiyun', "the seventh height," because it is seven hand-breadths above the earth. Every day the sun goes along under the arch, and returns at night on the upper side to the starting place.

There is another world under this, and it is like ours in everything—animals, plants, and people—save that the seasons are different. The streams that come down from the mountains are the trails by which we reach this underworld, and the springs at their heads are the doorways by which we enter it, but to do this one must fast and go to water and have one of the underground people for a guide. We know that the seasons in the underworld are different from ours, because the water in the springs is always warmer in winter and cooler in summer than the outer air.

When the animals and plants were first made—we do not know by whom—they were told to watch and keep awake for seven nights, just as young men now fast and keep awake when they pray to their medicine. They tried to do this, and nearly all were awake through the first night, but the next night several dropped off to sleep, and the third night others were asleep, and then others, until, on the seventh night, of all the animals only the owl, the panther, and one or two more were still awake. To these were given the power to see and to go about in the dark, and to make prey of the birds and animals which must sleep at night. Of the trees only the cedar, the pine, the spruce, the holly, and the laurel were awake to the end, and to them it was given to be always green and to be greatest for medicine, but to the others it was said: "Because you have not endured to the end you shall lose your hair every winter."

Men came after the animals and plants. At first there were only a brother and sister until he struck her with a fish and told her to multiply, and so it was. In seven days a child was born to her, and thereafter every seven days another, and they increased very fast until there was danger that the world could not keep them. Then it was made that a woman should have only one child in a year, and it has been so ever since.

The First Fire

In the beginning there was no fire, and the world was cold, until the Thunders (Ani'-Hyun'tikwala'ski), who lived up in Galun'lati, sent their lightning and put fire into the bottom of a hollow sycamore tree which grew on an island. The animals knew it was there, because they could see the smoke coming out at the top, but they could not get to it on account of the water, so they held a council to decide what to do. This was a long time ago.

Every animal that could fly or swim was anxious to go after the fire. The Raven offered, and because he was so large and strong they thought he could surely do the work, so he was sent first. He flew high and far across the water and alighted on the sycamore tree, but while he was wondering what to do next, the heat had scorched all his feathers black, and he was frightened and came back without the fire. The little Screech-Owl (Wa'huhu') volunteered to go, and reached the place safely, but while he was looking down into the hollow tree a blast of hot air came up and nearly burned out his eyes. He managed to fly home as best he could, but it was a long time before he could see well, and his eyes are red to this day. Then the Hooting Owl (*U'guku'*) and the Horned Owl (*Tskili'*) went, but by the time they got to the hollow tree the fire was burning so fiercely that the smoke nearly blinded them, and the ashes carried up by the wind made white rings about their eyes. They had to come home again without the fire, but with all their rubbing they were never able to get rid of the white rings.

Now no more of the birds would venture, and so little Uksu'hi snake, the black racer, said he would go through the water and bring back some fire. He swam across the island and crawled through the grass to the tree, and went in by a small hole at the bottom. The heat and smoke were too much for him, too, and after dodging about blindly over the hot ashes until he was almost on fire himself he managed by good luck to get out again at the same hole, but his body had been scorched black, and he has ever since had the habit of darting and doubling on his track as if trying to escape from close quarters. He came back, and the great blacksnake, Gule'gi, "The Climber," offered to go for fire. He swam over to the island and climbed up the tree on the outside, as the blacksnake always does, but when he put his head down into the hole the smoke choked him so that he fell into the burning stump, and before he could climb out again he was as black as the Uksu'hi.

Now they held another council, for still there was no fire, and the world was cold, but birds, snakes, and four-footed animals, all had some excuse for not going, because they were all afraid to venture near the burning sycamore, until at last Kanane'ski Amai'yehi (the Water Spider) said she would go. This is not the water spider that looks like a mosquito, but the other one, with black downy hair and red stripes on her body. She can run on top of the water or dive to the bottom, so there would be no trouble to get over to the island, but the question was, How could she bring back the fire? "I'll manage that," said the Water Spider; so she spun a thread from her body and wove it into a *tusti* bowl, which she fastened on her back. Then she crossed over to the island and through the grass to where the fire was still burning. She put one little coal of fire into her bowl, and came back with it, and ever since we have had fire, and the Water Spider still keeps her tusti bowl.

The Origin Of Disease And Medicine

In the old days quadrupeds, birds, fishes, and insects could all talk, and they and the human race lived together in peace and friendship. But as time went on the people increased so rapidly that their settlements spread over the whole earth and the poor animals found themselves beginning to be cramped for room. This was bad enough, but to add to their misfortunes man invented bows, knives, blowguns, spears, and hooks, and began to slaughter the larger animals, birds and fishes for the sake of their flesh or their skins, while the smaller creatures, such as the frogs and worms, were crushed and trodden upon without mercy, out of pure carelessness or contempt. In this state of affairs the animals resolved to consult upon measures for their common safety.

The bears were the first to meet in council in their townhouse in Kuwa'hi, the "Mulberry Place," and the old White Bear chief presided. After each in turn had made complaint against the way in which man killed their friends, devoured their flesh and used their skins for his own adornment, it was unanimously decided to begin war at once against the human race. Some-one asked what weapons man used to accomplish their destruction. "Bows and arrows, of course," cried all the bears in chorus. "And what are they made of?" was the next question. "The bow of wood and the string of our own entrails," replied one of the bears. It was then proposed that they make a bow and some arrows and see if they could not turn man's weapons against himself. So one bear got a nice piece of locust wood and another sacrificed himself for the good of the rest in order to furnish a piece of his entrails for the string. But when everything was ready and the first bear stepped up to make the trial it was found that in let-ting the arrow fly after drawing back the bow, his long claws caught the string and spoiled the shot. This was annoying, but another suggested that he could over-come the difficulty by cutting his claws, which was accordingly done, and on a second trial it was found that the arrow went straight to the mark. But here the chief, the old White Bear, interposed and said that it was necessary that they should have long claws in order to be able to climb trees. "One of us has already died to furnish the bow-string, and if we now cut off our claws we shall all have to starve together. It is better to trust to the teeth and claws which nature has given us, for it is evident that man's weapons were not intended for us."

No one could suggest any better plan, so the old chief dismissed the council and the bears disposed to their forest haunts without having concerted any means for preventing the increase of the human race. Had the result of the council been otherwise, we should now be at war with the bears, but as it is the hunter does not even ask the bear's pardon when he kills one.

The deer next held a council under their chief, the Little Deer, and after some deliberation resolved to inflict rheumatism upon every hunter who should kill one of their number, unless he took care to ask their pardon for the offense. They sent notice of their decision to the nearest settlement of Indians and told them at the same time how to make propitiation when necessity forced them to kill one of the deer tribe. Now, whenever the hunter brings down a deer, the Little Deer, who is swift as the wind and can not be wounded, runs quickly up to the spot and bending over the blood stains asks the spirit of the deer if it has heard the prayer of the hunter for pardon. If the reply be "Yes" all is well and the Little Deer goes on his way, but if the reply be in the negative he follows on the trail of the hunter, guided by the drops of blood on the ground, until he arrives at the cabin in the settlement, when the Little Deer enters invisibly and strikes the neglectful hunter with rheumatism so that he is rendered on the instant a helpless cripple. No hunter who has regard for his health ever fails to ask pardon of the deer for killing it, although some who have not learned the proper formula may attempt to turn aside the Little Deer from his pursuit by building a fire behind them in the trail.

Next came the fishes and reptiles, who had their own grievances against humanity. They held a joint council and determined to make their victims dream of snakes twining about them in slimy folds and blowing their fetid breath in their faces, or to make them dream of eating raw or decaying fish, so that they would lose appetite, sicken, and die. Thus it is that snake and fish dreams are accounted for.

Finally the birds, insects, and smaller animals came together for a like purpose, and the Grubworm presided over the deliberations. It was decided that each in turn should express an opinion and then vote on the question as to whether or not man should be deemed guilty. Seven votes were to be sufficient to condemn him. One after another denounced man's cruelty and injustice toward the other animals and voted in favor of his death. The Frog (wala'si) spoke first and said: "We must do something to check the increase of the race or people will become so numerous that we shall be crowded from off the earth. See how man has kicked me about because I'm ugly, as he says, until my back is covered with sores;" and here he showed the spots on his skin. Next came the Bird (tsi'skwa; no particular species is indicated), who condemned man because "he burns my feet off," alluding to the way in which the hunter barbecues birds by impaling them on a stick set over the fire, so that their feathers and tender feet are singed and burned. Others followed in the same strain. The Ground Squirrel alone ventured to say a word in behalf of man, who seldom hurt him because he was so small; but this so enraged the others that they fell upon the Ground Squirrel and tore him with their teeth and claws, and the stripes remain on his back to this day.

The assembly then began to devise and name various diseases, one after another, and had not their invention finally failed them not one of the human race would have been able to survive. The Grubworm in his place of honor hailed each new malady with delight, until at last they had reached the end of the list, . . .

When the plants, who were friendly to man, heard what had been done by the animals, they determined to defeat their evil designs. Each tree, shrub, and herb, down even to the grasses and mosses, agreed to furnish a remedy for some one of the diseases named, and each said: "I shall appear to help man when he calls upon me in his need." Thus did medicine originate, and the plants, every one of which has its use if we only knew it, furnish the antidote to counteract the evil wrought by the revengeful animals. When the doctor is in doubt what treatment to apply for the relief of a patient, the spirit of the plant suggests to him the proper remedy.

The Family

Although individual Cherokee families tended to be small, they were part of a much larger extended family called the clan. There were seven clans: Wolf, Deer, Bird, Paint, Wild Potato, Longhair, and the Blue Clan. Since families were traced through the mother's line, a man moved to a woman's town when they married, and if they were divorced, the man returned to his own clan, leaving the children and all possessions with the mother.

An Excerpt From *Slavery And The Evolution Of Cherokee Society 1540-1866* by Theda Perdue

The role of the mother in...the Cherokees' matrilineal kinship system...baffled whites until modern anthropologists made sense of it. In this kinship system, a person belonged to his mother's clan and his only kinsmen were those who could be traced through her—mother's mother, mother's sisters, the children of mother's sisters, and the most important and powerful man in a child's life, mother's brother. The primary responsibility for discipline and instruction in the arts of hunting and warfare rested not with a child's father but with his maternal uncle. . . .

Clan membership was essential to one's existence as a human being within Cherokee society because of

The traditional Cherokee house was a square structure built with stick-and-wattle construction. A common settlement would have anywhere between twenty and two hundred of these houses. The plaited mats of the walls were covered with mud and bark, and the roof was thatched. The house in the picture is only partially built. (Picture taken at the Qualla Arts and Crafts Mutual, Inc., in Cherokee, North Carolina.)

the pervasiveness of the kinship system. Since clans were divided into white or peace clans and red or war clans, a Cherokee's clan determined his political alignment and his role in society. Kinship governed social relationships, dictated possible marriage partners, designated friends and enemies and regulated comportment by indicating through terminology which kinsmen had to be respected and with which kinsmen one could be intimate. A Cherokee derived his rights from membership in a clan, and the clan protected those rights by promptly avenging any offense committed against a kinsman. If the actual perpetrator of a crime could not be apprehended, the clan of the wronged party retaliated against the offender's clan. The clan which adopted a captive became liable for his misdeeds as well as responsible for avenging wrongs done to him. To be without a clan in Cherokee society was to be without any rights, even the right to live.

Marriage Customs

The Cherokee, like many other Indian tribes, had fairly simple marriage customs. This article describes what courtship was probably like for Major Ridge (also called "the man who walks on the mountaintop" or The Ridge) and Susanna Wickett (Indian name Sehoya) when they married sometime around 1792. Major Ridge was described as a "farsighted" leader of the Cherokees, and his son, John Ridge, followed in his footsteps.

An Excerpt From *Cherokee Tragedy*
The Story of the Ridge Family and of the Decimation of a People
by Thurman Wilkins

As The Ridge still followed the old Cherokee customs at the time, he may have effected the engagement in the traditional manner, by killing a deer and taking it to the lodge of Susanna's parents to indicate that he was a good provider. In that case she would have accepted his suit by cooking him a meal. But Cherokee courtship was not all practicality; there was also covert sentiment, according to General Sam Dale, a hard-bitten white trader and Indian fighter, who gave a romantic picture of Cherokee wooing: "An Indian maid, when a warrior approaches, bends her head like a drooping leaf. It is only in the deepest recesses, when no others are near, that her lover sees the luster of her eyes, or even the blushes that mantle her cheeks."

The Ridge's courtship seems to have gone well. The pair probably went before a conjurer for a prediction on the course of the marriage, and his words presumably were favorable.

As for the marriage itself, the traditional rite was simple. With several companions, the groom received a ceremonial meal in a lodge on one side of the town house, while the bride, similarly waited on, was feted in the house on the other side. At the close of the banquets the men and women of the village took their respective places at opposite sides of the town house. Then the attendants let the bride and groom into the council chamber, where they stood as far apart as possible. A woman relative of the groom, in the absence of his mother, handed him a ham of venison and a blanket. At the same time the bride's mother gave her an ear of corn and a blanket also. The two young people then walked slowly toward each other and, on meeting, exchanged the venison and the corn and put the blankets together, an act which symbolized their promise of living together in the same house, the man providing the meat, the woman the corn. It was customary then for the town chief to pronounce "the blankets joined" —that is, the couple was married. When The Ridge led Susanna from the town house (if, indeed, they observed the ancient custom), both held ends of the blankets, while he carried the corn and she the venison. Tradition would decree that he lead her to a new cabin, in Pine Log, no doubt a typical Indian shelter, made of logs, with a bark roof and an earthen floor. The fireplace would have lain in the center of the room under a hole in the roof to serve as sole chimney.

Games And Recreation

Cherokee children, like the children of today, enjoyed playing games. Although a great deal of the Cherokee culture has been lost through the years, some descriptions of games and recreation remain. Today, in the Cherokee schools, the children are taught from an early age the traditions of their culture so that they will not be lost again.

An Excerpt From *Cherokee Plants And Their Uses — A 400 Year History* by Paul B. Hamel & Mary U. Chiltoskey

Among the games the Cherokees played, marbles and Chung-ke were outdoor games; while the popular butterbean game could be played indoors. These and other games the people played were less an occasion for competition than for socializing.

Hardly any Cherokee was without marbles in his pocket. Made of pottery clay and hardened in the fire, they gave a person the chance to play and bet with his friends during leisure time. Small marbles could be fired while moist; if larger they had to be thoroughly dry before firing. These were usually made several at a time, in case one or more broke during the firing. Changing the kind of clay, and the woods used in the fire altered the color of the marbles.

The Chung-ke game was played by men or boys using stout sticks and a special disc, the Chung-ke stone. The stone was about five inches in diameter, and concave on both sides. One player rolled the stone on its edge down an incline onto a flat area. The others threw their sticks at it as it rolled; knocking the stone over was an automatic win. Otherwise the player whose stick was closest to the stone when it stopped rolling was the winner.

The butterbean game was another pastime. Two teams of any number could play and the equipment was simple. The game was played with six half-butterbeans, twenty four corn kernels as counters, and a flat basket about eighteen inches square and approximately two and a half inches deep. The baskets were likely to have been made of the inner hickory bark, cane, or oak splits.

To play the butterbean game, a person put the six half-butterbeans in the basket, flipped them into the air, and caught them. Each flip that scored gave the scorer another turn. Only three combinations were counted: 1. all flat, light sides — six points; 2. all round, dark sides — four points; 3. a single side of one color and five of the other color — two points. The game began with all the counters in a neutral pot and ended when one of the teams had all the counters. The game brought people together for enjoyment.

Originally in midwinter and more recently at Christmas time, this game came into its own. On Christmas eve it was traditional for the men to play against the women. The losers gathered wood for the women to cook Christmas dinner. Winners were entitled to use soot to smut the losers' faces.

Cherokee children played with toys that imitated their adult roles. The girls had cornshuck or rag dolls and toy Ka-no-na's; the boys had small bows, blowguns, and ballsticks. Their play taught them their adult roles.

Arbitration

The ball-play, A-ne-tsa (little brother to war), was important to Cherokee people because it involved religious ritual and had political overtones. Coosawattee in north Georgia commemorates the peaceful settlement of a land dispute between the Cherokee and Creek nations by ball-play. The Cherokees won. To this day, the place is called Coosawattee, meaning the "old country of the Creeks."

Each team has two managers, called drivers because of the long hickory switches they carry, who are responsible for making sure the few rules are not violated. The object of the game is to throw or carry the ball through a goal marked by two green saplings. The goals lie about one hundred twenty yards apart on flat open ground. The game is played until one team scores twelve points. There is no time limit.

Every player carries two hickory ballsticks, shaped like long handled miniature tennis rackets strung with leather, Indian hemp or inner hickory bark. The sticks are approximately eighteen inches long. Players are required to use these to pick the ball up from the ground. The ball was about the size of a golfball, made of leather stuffed with deer hair; today it is made of rubber.

James Mooney's book, *Myths of the Cherokee and Sacred Formulas of the Cherokees*, contains information about

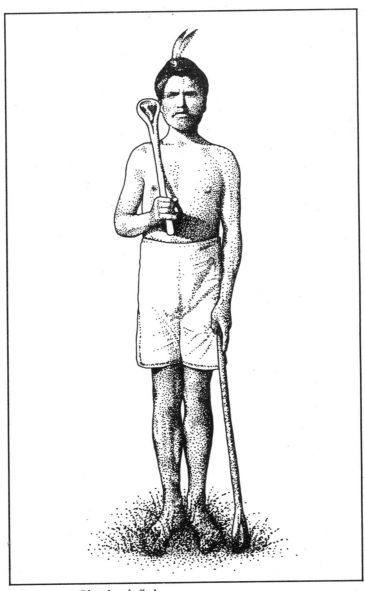

Sawanu gi, a Cherokee ball-player

the rigorous training program of those early players. ...Workouts were conducted by a medicine man who used various plant materials in conjunction with the prescribed rituals. The men rubbed their limbs with preparations from such plants as the slippery elm to make themselves strong and slippery. The players, with the aid and direction of the medicine man prepared themselves spiritually, mentally, and physically.

Betting on the game was a serious affair and often bitterly contested. For this reason betting on the game and finally the game itself was outlawed for several decades in this century by white authorities.

Inventing The Alphabet

There are many books describing the life of Sequoyah. In his book, Grant Foreman relates the interesting story of how Sequoyah (also called George Guess) invented the Cherokee alphabet. To do this, Grant Foreman used the lecture notes of Samuel Lorenzo Knapp, who interviewed Sequoyah.

An Excerpt From "Sequoyah"
by Grant Foreman

Sequoyah was led to think on the subject of writing the Cherokee language by a conversation which took place at the Cherokee town of Sauta. Some young men were remarking on the wonderful and superior talents of the white people. One of the company said that white men could put a talk on a piece of paper and send it any distance, and it would be perfectly understood by those who would receive it.

All admitted that this was indeed an art far beyond the reach of the Indian, and they were utterly at a loss to conceive in what way it was done. Sequoyah, after listening awhile in silence to the conversation, observed, "you are all fools; why the thing is very easy; I can do it myself." And taking up a flat stone which lay near him, he began making words on it with a pen. After a few minutes he told them what he had written, by making a mark for each word. This produced a laugh and the conversation on that subject ended. This was enough however, to start the inventive Sequoyah to serious speculation on the subject.

He had to contend with the prejudices of the Cherokees who tried to convince him that God had made a great distinction between the white and the red man by relating to him the following tradition: In the beginning God created the Indian, the real or genuine man, and the white man. The Indian was the elder and in his hands the Creator placed a book; in the hands of the other he placed a bow and arrow, with a command that they should both make good use of them. The Indian was very slow in receiving the book, and appeared so indifferent about it that the white man came and stole it from him when his attention was directed another way. He was then compelled to take the bow and arrow, and gain his subsistence by pursuing the chase. He had thus forfeited the book which his Creator had placed in his hands and which now of right belonged to his white brother.

The narration of this story however, was not sufficient to convince Sequoyah, and to divert him from his great purpose. After the interview at Sauta, he went home, procured materials, and in earnest began to paint the Cherokee language on paper. His labors were further described by Mr. Knapp:

"From the cries of wild beasts, from the talents of the mocking-bird, from the voices of his children and his companions, he knew that feelings and passions were conveyed by different sounds, from one intelligent being to another. The thought struck him to ascertain all the sounds in the Cherokee language. His own ear

George Guess (Sequoyah)

was not remarkably discriminating, and he called to his aid the more acute ears of his wife and children. He found great assistance from them. When he thought that he had distinguished all the different sounds in their language, he attempted to use his pictorial signs, images of birds and beasts, to convey these sounds to others or to mark them in his own mind. He soon dropped this method, as difficult or impossible, and tried arbitrary signs, without any regard to appearances, except such as might assist him in recollecting them, and distinguishing them from each other."

Sequoyah at first thought of no way but to make a character for each word. He pursued this plan for about a year, in which time he had put down several thousand characters. He was then convinced that the object was not to be obtained in that way. But he was not to be discouraged. He firmly believed there was some way in which the Cherokee language could be expressed on paper, and after trying several other methods, he at length hit upon the idea of dividing the words into parts or syllables. He had not proceeded far on this plan, when he found to his great satisfaction, that the same characters would apply in different words, and that the number would be comparatively few.

After putting down and learning all the syllables that he could think of, he would listen to speeches, and the conversation of strangers, and whenever a word occurred which had a part or a syllable in it, which he had not before thought of, he "would recollect it until he had made a character for it." In this way he soon discovered all the syllables in the language. After commencing upon the last plan, it is believed he completed his system in about a month. He adopted a number of English letters which he took from the spelling book then in his possession. "At first these symbols were very numerous; and when he got so far as to think his invention was nearly accomplished he had about 200 characters in his alphabet. By the aid of his daughter, who seemed to enter into the genius of his labors, he reduced them at last, to 86, the number he now uses.

"He then set to work to make these characters more comely to the eye, and succeeded. As yet he had not

ᏣᎳᎩ ᏗᏫᏁᎢᏍᏗ
(Cherokee Words)

English	Cherokee	Pronunciation
Amen	ᎡᎺᏅ	e-me-nv
baby	ᎤᏍᏗᎦ	u-s-di-ga
bad	ᎤᏲᎢ	u-yo-i
bed	ᎦᏂᏏ	ga-ni-si
bird	ᏥᏍᏆ	tsi-s-qua
boy	ᎠᏧᏣ	a-tsu-tsa
bread	ᎦᏚ	ga-du
bridge	ᎠᏒᏥ	a-sv-tsi
cat	ᏪᏌ	we-sa
chair	ᎦᏍᎩᎶ	ga-s-gi-lo
chicken	ᏣᏔᎦ	tsa-ta-ga
corn	ᏎᎷ	se-lu
day	ᎢᎦ	i-ga
dog	ᎩᎵ	gi-li
earth	ᎡᎶᎯᏃ	e-lo-hi-no
father	ᎡᏙᏓ	e-do-da
flower	ᎱᏥᎸᎭ	hu-tsi-lv-ha
forest	ᎠᏙᎯ	a-do-hi
friend	ᎣᎩᎾᎵᎢ	o-gi-na-li-i
girl	ᎠᎨᏳᏣ	a-ge-yu-tsa
God	ᎡᏙᏓ	e-do-da

Courtesy of the *Rome New Tribune*, Rome, Georgia, Pastimes Cherokee Indian Edition, August 1990.

the knowledge of the pen as an instrument, but made his characters on a piece of bark with a knife or nail. At this time he sent to the Indian agent, or some trader in the nation, for paper and pen. His ink was easily made from some of the bark of the forest trees, whose coloring [properties] he had previously known; and after seeing the construction of the pen, he soon learned to make one; but at first he made it without a slit; this inconvenience was, however, quickly removed by his sagacity."

During the time he was occupied in inventing the alphabet, he was strenuously opposed by all his friends and neighbors. He was frequently told that he was throwing away his time and labor, and that none but a delirious person or an idiot would do as he did. But this did not discourage him. He would listen to the expostulations of his friends, and then deliberately light his pipe, pull his spectacles over his eyes, and sit down to his work, without attempting to vindicate his conduct.

"After completing his system, he found much difficulty in persuading the people to learn it. Nor could he succeed until he went to the Cherokees in Arkansas and taught a few persons there, one of whom wrote a letter to some of his friends in the Cherokee Nation east of the Mississippi and sent it by Mr. Guess, who read it to the people on his return.

"This letter excited much curiosity: here was talk in the Cherokee language, which had come all the way from the Arkansas sealed up in paper, and yet it was very plain. This convinced many that Mr. Guess' mode of writing would be of some use. Several persons immediately determined to try to learn. They succeeded in a few days, and from this it spread all over the nation, and the Cherokees (who as a people had always been illiterate) were, in the course of a few months, without school, or expense of time, or money, able to read and write in their own language.

Ode To Sequoyah
by Alex Posey, Creek Indian Poet

The names of Watie and Boudinot—
    The valiant warrior and gifted sage—
And other Cherokees, may be forgot,
    But thy name shall descend to every age;
The mysteries enshrouding Cadmus' name
Cannot obscure thy claim to fame.

The people's language cannot perish—nay,
    When from the face of this great continent
Inevitable doom hath swept away
    The last memorial—the last fragment
Of tribes,—some scholar learned shall pore
Upon thy letters, seeking lore.
Some bard shall lift a voice in praise of thee,
    In moving numbers tell the world how men
Scoffed thee, hissed thee, charged with lunacy!
    And who could not give 'nough honor when
At length, in spite of jeers, of want and need,
Thy genius shaped a dream into a deed.

By cloud-capped summits in the boundless west,
    Or mighty river rolling to the sea,
Where'er thy footsteps led thee on that quest,
    Unknown, rest thee, illustrious Cherokee.

Education

In this section there are three descriptions of the education of the Cherokee children. The first tells of the traditional style of education, through dances and stories; the second relates information about the missionary schools of the early 1800s, and the third describes the life of the Indians who were sent to the missionary school at Cornwall, Connecticut.

An Excerpt From *Cherokee Plants And Their Uses — A 400 Year History*
by Paul B. Hamel & Mary U. Chiltoskey

Dances are likely to have re-enacted historical events and generally instructed people about their environment and the things in it. Special dances required such equipment as masks, costumes, and musical instruments; gourd or turtleshell rattles and drums of hemlock or buckeye covered with ground hog skin were used. Many dances were totally lost during the last century.

Dances remembered by folks and still in use in the 1970s are: Ball, Bear, Beaver, Buffalo, Booger, Eagle, Friendship, Green Corn, Partridge (Quail). The dances show us that Cherokee women often danced while their men danced, though seldom with them. During the time when traditional Cherokee society was intact, education surpassed recreation as a primary reason for dancing. Masks were usually made of buckeye wood or other materials that could be shaped quite easily. Wands used in the eagle dance were made of cane or sourwood.

Though children lacked the structured schooling of the twentieth century, their learning opportunities were constant. They began by imitating adults and as their skills progressed they were given new goals. Story time was one form of instruction. The following is one of Mary Chiltoskey's favorite stories about one of the plants found in this region.

"Before selfishness came into the world — that was a long time ago — the Cherokee people were happy sharing the hunting and fishing places with their neighbors. All this changed when Selfishness came into the world and men began to quarrel. The Cherokees quarreled with tribes on the east. Finally the chiefs of several tribes met in council to try to settle the dispute. They smoked the pipe and continued to quarrel for seven days and seven nights. This displeased the Great Spirit because people are not supposed to smoke the pipe until they make peace. As he looked upon the old men with heads bowed, he decided to do something to remind people to smoke the pipe only at the time they make peace.

The Great Spirit turned the old men into grayish flowers we now call 'Indian Pipes' and made them grow where friends and relatives have quarreled. He made the smoke hang over these mountains until all people all over the world learn to live together in peace.

Journal of Cherokee Studies
Cherokee Education In Missionary Schools
From *The New York Spectator*,
November 23, 1821, (New York, N.Y.)

(Editor's note: Except for the few wealthy Cherokees who could afford to send their children to private schools, or hire tutors, most of the nation were dependent on schools established by missionaries. The following article is a brief report concerning the best known mission school which was founded by the American Board of Commissioners for Foreign Missions at Brainerd.)

Extract from the report of the Rev. A. Hoyt, of the progress of the schools in the Cherokee Nation under his superintendance, date "Brainerd, Cherokee Nation, Oct. 1, 1821

"There are, belonging to the two schools, taught in this place, ninety-six Cherokee children of both sexes, about two-third males—all of whom are boarded, and many of them clothed, at the expense of the mission. Many promising children we have been obliged to reject or put by until those now in school should be prepared to go out and make room for them, as we cannot accommodate, and profitably teach more than we have had. Of those who attended school last year, three have finished their course and left the institution, and six others have left the school who could read and write. Twenty-four have entered the past year.

"At the local schools we board but few scholars, not to exceed eight or ten at each school, and at present, not more than four or five at Taloney. As some of the scholars who board at home, have a great distance to walk, they are not all constant attendants, and the number of those who attend at all, is not so great as when the schools first commenced. The average number attending the local schools, the year past, has been between forty and fifty. Public workship is attended, at each of these schools, on the Sabbath, at which numbers of the parents, as well as the children, attend, and some have made a public profession of the Christian religion.

"The children of the schools continue to manifest an aptness to learn, a willingness to labour, and a readiness to submit to all the rules of the school. The Cherokees, we think, are fast advancing towards civilized life. [They] generally manifest an ardent desire for literary and religious instruction."

Education Of John Ridge
An Excerpt From *Cherokee Tragedy*

The term was several weeks old when John and his comrades reached the school toward the end of November. It was so late in the season that the maple tree in front of the schoolhouse was bare and ceased to be of shelter to the small gambrel-roofed building of one and a half stories that stood near the Cornwall green. Long known as the "Academy," the building had been given to the American Board of Commissioners by the town in the previous year, along with fourteen acres of land that centered on the "Commons" or steward's house on West Road, and eighty-six more that lay on the northerly slope of Colt's Foot Mountain. The town of Cornwall, which sprawled at the mountain's base, was an agricultural community, a cluster of neat, trim farmhouses about the village green, on the east bank of the Housatonic. The place had been selected for the Foreign Mission School because of its

40

The Foreign Mission School, Cornwall, Connecticut.

sheltered location and its reputation for general health-fulness. An English visitor would describe its location as "a deep retired romantic valley" whose southern approach, "for three or four miles, lay through a natural grove of hemlock, spruce. . .and cedar, which hung over [the] path, and whose matted boughs and dark green leaves formed a fine contrast with the new fallen snow." . . .

The program at the Foreign Mission School was designed to allow the devil no chance through idleness. After arising early in their quarters under the gambrel roof, the boys would gather for morning prayer at the ringing of a bell at 6 A.M. They would first read a chapter in the New Testament, each taking a verse in turn. Then an older student would lead the devotions of the group. After breakfast in the Commons came the morning stint of work in the garden near that building, matched by another before the evening meal. The students had practice also in mechanics and other manual work, Thomas Basel later becoming a blacksmith in the Cherokee Nation, putting to use some of the techniques he had learned at Cornwall. The boys, though probably before John's arrival, had laid "with odd crookedness" the pipe that consisted of strips of lead folded around and soldered along the seam to conduct water from a nearby spring to the Commons and the principal's house. There were also fields to be ploughed, for which the townspeople lent plows and spans of oxen, the Reverend Mr. Stone of the First Congregational Church saying a prayer before the first furrow was begun. In summer the boys chopped wood on the side of Colt's Foot Mountain for the winter months ahead. Physical labor thus formed a definite part of the school's program.

Several hours before noon and most of the afternoon were devoted to study and recitations in the classroom. The students worked at various levels, on varying subjects, with differing rates of speed. Because of their groundings at Spring Place and Brainerd the Cherokees forged ahead, and before long John and Elias were studying the most advanced subjects in the curriculum. In 1821 Daggett reported to Dr. Jedidiah Morse, the eminent geographer at Yale College, whose son Samuel would become even more famous, that the two Cherokee cousins had "studied Geography extensively, Rhetoric, Surveying, Ecclesiastical and Common History, three books in the Aeneid, two orations of Cicero, and are attending to Natural Philosophy."

Much of each evening was devoted to prayer.

John Ridge

Mr. Daggett felt deeply "the vast responsibility of a minister of Christ," and the boys' souls were as much the objects of his attentions as their minds. There was no relaxation of the religious emphasis. After a week of prayer and Bible reading the boys were expected to hear Timothy Stone's sermons twice on Sunday at the First Church, where they were restricted to one far corner, possibly the same corner in which the back of a gallery pew recorded a critical evaluation of the

young man who had recently become the assistant
principal:

> The eloquence of Herman Vaill
> Would make the stoutest sinner quail.

The couplet was followed by another of firm dissent:

> The hissing goose has far more sense
> Than Vaill with all his eloquence.

At the church one day in May each year the Foreign
Mission School would hold an anniversary exercise in
which the students were exhibited to the townspeople.
In 1820 there were thirteen declamations in a half-
dozen languages, John leading off the program with a
speech in English, followed by Elias. A young lady of
the town would later remember: "The Indian pupils
appeared so genteel and graceful on the stage that the
white pupils seemed uncouth beside them. The Indians
sang and prayed in their native tongues; when they
prayed they knelt, clasped both hands and held them
up. When they sang, they sat in a row, and all waved
their hands simultaneously." The Cherokee youths completed the program of 1820 with a dialogue concerning
the problem of removal to Arkansas. In 1821 they cli-
maxed the anniversary by staging a war council of the
Arkansas Cherokees ready to fight their Osage neighbors. They won additional friends for the school, creating
favorable impressions even among those who had
hitherto looked askance at the program.

Upon A Watch
by John Ridge (February 4, 1819)

Little monitor, by thee,
Let me learn what I should be:
Learn the round of life to fill,
Thou canst gentle hints impart,
How to regulate the heart.
When I wind thee up at night
Mark each fault and set thee right,
Let me search my bosom too,
And my daily thoughts review,
Mark the movements of my mind
Nor be easy when I find
Latent errors rise to view,
Till all be regular and true.

New Echota

Journal of Cherokee Studies
A Visit To New Echota
From *The New York American*,
July 16, 1830, (New York, N.Y.)

(Editor's note: Life went on in the Cherokee Nation in spite of the growing crises regarding removal. This article describes the visit of a New England couple to New Echota, the Cherokee capitol, to spend some time with their daughter and her husband. Their daughter, Harriet, was the wife of Elias Boudinot, a young Cherokee intellectual and editor of the Cherokee Phoenix.)

The Cherokee Indians.—Gettysburg, (PA) July 6—We had a visit on Friday last from a gentleman (Col. Gold, of Connecticut,) and his lady, who were on their return from the Cherokee Nation, where they have spent the last 8 months, on a visit to their daughter, who is married to E. Boudinot, Editor of the "Cherokee Phoenix." A great variety of interesting information relative to those people was communicate to us—all tending to establish the fact, that civilization has made a most unexampled progress in the Nation. The great body of the Cherokees live in comfort, and many of them in affluence and splendor. Since Col. G. has been amongst them, he has witnessed the clearing of lands, erection of buildings, and improvements of various descriptions, progressing with steady pace. The education of their youth is becoming an object of desire and attention; and religious instruction and general

This is a reconstruction of the 1827 Cherokee Phoenix printing office located at the New Echota State Historic Site. The newspaper was printed weekly and distributed both in the United States and Europe. Copies of the newspaper can be seen at some research libraries in their microform departments.

This is an original Cherokee Indian building built around 1800. It was owned by James Vann and used as a store, tavern, and inn. It was originally located near Gainsville, Georgia, but was moved to New Echota State Historic Site (Georgia) in 1955.

Photograph by: R. C. Meyers, Jr.

In later years the Cherokee nation had a three-judge Supreme Court in their capitol at New Echota. This reconstruction of their 1829 Supreme Court building can be found at the New Echota State Historic Site.

information is gradually finding its way through the community.

A large proportion of families manufacture woollen and cotton goods for domestic use, and also for exchange for other articles from abroad; and the wheel and the loom meet your eye in almost every house. Col. G. had with him specimens of their manufactured woollen and cotton goods, which were really excellent, and will bear comparison with those of cotton manufactured here. Our informant states also, that their roads are in fine order—that he was able to travel with his carriage through every part of the Nation. He also attended the meeting of their General Council; and was astonished at the order and regularity of their business, and the talented [sic] displayed by the members. As respects their present perilous situation, they are firm, relying with confidence upon the uprightness of the decision of the Supreme Court of the United States—before which tribunal they hope to have the question brought.

Sample of the Cherokee Phoenix, America's first bilingual newspaper.

CONSTITUTION OF THE CHE-
ROKEE NATION,

Formed by a Convention of Delegates from the several Districts, at New E-chota, July 1827.

WE, THE REPRESENTATIVES of the people of the CHEROKEE NATION in Convention assembled, in order to establish justice, ensure tranquility, promote our common welfare, and secure to ourselves and our posterity the blessings of liberty; acknowledging with humility and gratitude the goodness of the sovereign Ruler of the Universe, in offering us an opportunity so favorable to the design, and imploring his aid and direction in its accomplishment, do ordain and establish this Constitution for the Government of the Cherokee Nation.

ARTICLE I.

Sec. 1. THE BOUNDARIES of this nation, embracing the lands solemnly guarantied and reserved forever to the Cherokee Nation by the Treaties concluded with the United States, are as follows; and shall forever hereafter remain unalterably the same—to wit—Beginning on the North Bank of Tennessee River at the upper part of the Chickasaw old fields; thence along the main channel of said river, including all the islands therein, to the mouth of the Hiwassee river, thence up the main channel of said river, including Islands, to the first hill which closes in on said river, about two miles above Hiwassee old Town; thence along the ridge which divides the waters of the Hiwassee and little Tellico, to the Tennessee river at Tallassee; thence along the main channel, including Islands, to the junction of the Cowee and Nanteyalee; thence along the ridge in the fork of said river, to the top of the blue ridge; thence along the blue ridge to the Unicoy Turnpike road; thence by a straight line to the main source of the Chestatee; thence along its main chan-

---

(Cherokee syllabary column)

ᏣᎳᎩᏱ ᎤᎾᏙᏗ ᎬᏗ ᎤᎬᏩᎵ.

ᏣᎳ ᏔᎢᏏᏯ ᎠᏁᎶᎢᏍᎩ ᎤᎵᏁᎯᎥ, ᏗᎦᎸᎳ ᎠᎵᏍᎪ.

ᎠᏎ ᎡᏂᏱ ᏙᎯᎵᎠᏈ ᎠᏏᎢ ᎠᎠᏱᏫ, ᎬᏫ ᎤᎤᎴᎿ ᎠᏯᏗᎦᎵ, ᏍᏆᎯ ᏚᏯᎳᏔᏫᎳ, ᏗᎠ ᎤᏍᎵᎢᎦᏍᏗ Ꮽ ᎬᏫ ᎠᏏᎢ ᎨᏯᏉᏯᎵᎵᎢᏌ, ᎤᏍᎭᎥ ᏍᏯ ᎤᎵᎠᎵᎠᎵᎭ ᏯᏛ ᎨᏳᏟ ᎯᏈᎡ ᎯᎩ, ᏗᎢ ᎩᎯᎭ ᎤᎾᏫ ᎤᎩᏯ ᎤᎦᎳᎵ ᎨᎵᎭᏆᎵᎾᎵᎭ, ᎨᏳ ᏫᎤᏣᎢ, ᎠᏗ ᎤᎾᎦᎳᎢ ᎬᏫ ᎤᎬᏐ ᎤᎪᏛᎾ. ᏗᎤᏬᏫᎵᎢᎶ ᏒᎢ, ᎯᎴᏊ ᎤᏤᎪᎦᎢ, ᏍᏂᎯ ᏣᏔᎵ; ᏗᎢ ᎤᎪᎴᏆᎵᎢ ᎣᎭᏯ ᏔᎦᎳᎯᏛ ᎯᎩ ᎠᏗ ᎤᎭᏯ ᏔᎦᏣᎵ ᎨᏯᏉᎵᎵᎵ ᎯᎮᎯᏐᎵᎭ, ᏗᎢ ᎤᎭᏯ ᏍᏯᎠᎢᏎᎵᎭ, ᏗᎢ ᎤᎵᎭᎵᎭ, ᎤᎯᏫᎭᏈ.

I.

1. ᏗᎬᎦᎵ ᎯᏓᎬᎵᎢᎵ ᏙᎾᏫᏱ ᎤᎤᎢᎤᏆ ᏍᎵᏣ, ᎤᏂᎨᎦᎳ ᏚᎦᎭᎵᏆᏂᎵ ᏍᎦᎵᎰᎵᎮ, ᏗᎢ ᎤᎦᎵ. ᎠᏂᎦ ᎯᎩ, ᎤᏤᏛᎵᎠ ᏎᎤᎵᎦᎵᏛᎦᎵᎪ-, ᎠᏗ ᎤᎦᎵ; ᏗᎢ ᎤᎭᏯᏛᎵ ᎦᎳᏛᎵ ᎭᎵᎦᎵ ᎤᎵᎦᏓᎵᎠᎵ ᎯᎮᎵᎢᎦᎵᎭᎡ ᎡᎵᏨᎵᏌ.Ꭲ. ᎯᎵᏍᏛ ᎤᎭᎡᎦᎵᎢᎤ ᎤᏬᎵ ᎤᎪᏈᏔ ᎠᎵᎤᎭᎵᎸᎾᎵ-ᎣᏱ, ᎤᎭᏯ ᎤᎯᎵᎡᎾᏍᏆᎢᎶ, ᎯᏍᎵᎢ ᏗᎢᏍᏈ ᏍᏆᏍᏍ ᎬᏫ ᎠᎵ.

A closer look at English and Cherokee, side-by-side.

50

In Defense Of The Cherokees

Letter Of S. A. Worcester
From the *Cherokee Phoenix And Indians' Advocate*,
October 28, 1829, Volume II, Number 29

New Echota, C.N.
Sept. 23, 1829

To the Editor of the Charleston Observer.

Rev. and Dear Sir, — Your paper of Sept. 5th, having this week fallen into my hands, I read with pain a statement respecting the state of the Cherokee Indians, which too manifestly contravenes the representations often made public from Missionaries residing in the nation. The statement to which I refer is the following, "We have been informed on good authority, that, so far as the Cherokees are concerned, while a few are growing wealthy, the majority of the people are actually growing poorer and poorer every year." This statement is accompanied with no responsible name, though said to be made on good authority. I have now resided among the Cherokees in the capacity of a Missionary, for nearly four years, and have had some opportunity of judging respecting their state; and I have no hesitation in resting my reputation for veracity or judgement on the assertion, that the statement quoted above is altogether without foundation. On the contrary, the condition of the majority of the people, not including those who may be termed wealthy, is, in point of property, constantly improving and never more rapidly than at the present time.

There is another editorial remark in the same article, repeating which, I beg the indulgence of a few words of comment. You say, "though a few may feel the sanction of an oath, the majority of them—unless they are greatly slandered—utterly disregard it." This remark relates to the Creeks and Cherokees. With the Creeks I am not acquainted; but in regard to the Cherokees I must say, then they *are* greatly slandered. There is no foundation for the remark in the character of the people. The magistrates of the nation are in the habit of administering oaths in their courts of justice, and I am persuaded that nothing has occurred to indicate that they are less regarded than among their more civilized neighbors.

I am sorry, dear Sir, that these unfounded reports should have reached your ears, especially through any such channels as to give them credence, and make your paper, respectable as it is, the means of circulating them.

> With much esteem.
> Your fellow-laborer in the
>   Gospel,
> S. A. Worcester

Georgia Pardons Two
Who Fought Treatment Of Cherokees

From the Lowell Sun, Lowell, Massachusetts
November 26, 1992, p. 47.

Atlanta (AP) — More than 160 years after Georgia officials ignored a direct order from the U.S. Supreme Court to stop actions leading up to the infamous Trail of Tears, the state is admitting it made a mistake.

Officials yesterday formally pardoned two missionaries jailed when they fought the state's seizure of Cherokee Indian land.

"This is one of many injustices done, but it's something that we could do something about," said Marsha Bailey, spokeswoman for the state Board of Pardons and Paroles. "It was a miscarriage of justice."

The pardon says it "acts to remove a stain on the history of criminal justice in Georgia" and acknowledges the state usurped Cherokee sovereignty and ignored the Supreme Court.

A legislator and Cherokee descendant called the pardon a sign that Georgia finally realizes the scope of its mistreatment of the Cherokee.

"If we ever had political prisoners in this state or this nation, these two were the best examples," said Rep. Bill Dover, chief executive of the Georgia Tribe of Eastern Cherokee.

Samuel Austin Worcester and Elihu Butler were sentenced to four years in jail in 1831 for residing in the Cherokee Nation without a license. A law was enacted to try to stop the two from protesting the state's seizure of Cherokee land in northwest Georgia.

Until 1828, the Cherokee Nation was considered a sovereign foreign country, with its land off limits to settlers. But the next year, gold was discovered in Dahlonega and Georgia seized much of the land and abolished Cherokee sovereignty.

Worcester and Butler, who lived at the Cherokee capitol of New Echota, attracted national attention to the Indians' cause. To muzzle them, the state required all white men living on Cherokee land to obtain a state license. Worcester and Butler refused and were convicted of "high misdemeanor."

The missionaries appealed to the U.S. Supreme Court. In 1832, Chief Justice John Marshall declared Georgia had no constitutional right to extend any state laws over the Cherokee, including seizing their land, and must release the missionaries.

But Georgia ignored the ruling. The missionaries spent 16 months doing hard labor as part of a chain gang, Dover said.

They were released in time to join the Trail of Tears, when Georgia forced up to 17,000 Cherokees to move west. Thousands died of cold and starvation during the march, but the missionaries made it to Oklahoma and continued their work among Cherokee there.

The Cherokee

From the *Philadelphia Christian Advocate*,
as printed in the *Cherokee Phoenix And Indians' Advocate*,
June 5, 1830, Volume III, Number 7

...Proud was his spirit, fierce, untamed and free,
  Scorning to crouch to pain, from death to flee,
With feeling suited to his savage state,
  Faithful alike to friendship or to hate,
Seeking no meed beyond a warrior's fame,
  And fearing nought except a coward's shame.

These wilds were his; amidst his chosen dell,
  Where clustering wildflowers fringed the
    gushing well,
His hut was reared; and there, at closing day,
  He heard his children's laughter-shout of play,
While, weary with the chase, his limbs were laid
  In listless rest, beneath the oak tree's shade

Then o'er the ocean-sea the white man came
  Held to his lips the cup of liquid flame,
With smooth, false words, and bold encrouching
    hand,
  Wrenched from the Cherokee his father's land,
Still on his fast receding footsteps prest,
  And urged him onwards to the distant West,
'Till all the precincts of his narrowed ground,
  Were closely hemmed with cultured life around;
And burning cottages and mangled slain,
  Had marked war's footsteps o'er the ravaged plain.

Wearied, at length, the pale browed stranger swore,
  To seek the Indian's hunting ground no more;

Treaties and oaths the solemn compact sealed,
  And plenty crowned once more the blood stained
    field.
Then o'er the red men's altered nature smiles
  A kindlier spirit, and a soul more mild;
Bright knowledge poured its sunlight o'er his mind,
  His feelings softened, and his heart refined.

    . . .

Then tell us, ye, who have the power to save,
  Shall all his hopes be crushed in one wide grave?
Shall lawless force, with rude, remorseless hand,
  Drive out the Indian from his father's land,
Burst all the ties that bind the heart to home,
  And thrust him forth, 'mid distant wilds to roam?
Oh no! to mercy's pleading voice give ear,
  The wak'ning wrath of outraged justice fear,
Stain not with broken faith our country's name,
  Nor weigh her tresses to the dust with shame!
Remember yet the solemn pledge you gave,
  And lift the potent arm, to shield and save!

Definitions

bicameral – composed of two houses or branches

Booger – "Boogie man," called s-g-li in Cherokee

Cadmus – A prince in Greek mythology who killed a dragon and then planted its teeth, which grew into an army of men who fought each other until only five survived.

comportment – bearing; the way one carries oneself

encrouching (encroaching) – to intrude gradually upon the domain or rights of another

Ka-no-na's – long-handled tool used to crush corn into meal

meed – a gift or reward

renascence – rebirth, revival

shunning – deliberately avoid a person

wattle and daub – an interweaving of sticks and twigs, plastered with mud or clay.

Bibliography

Cherokee Phoenix, Oklahoma State Library Archives Division, 1828-1834.

Foreman, Grant, *Sequoyah*, University of Oklahoma Press, 1938.

Hamel, Paul B. and Mary U. Chiltoskey, *Cherokee Plants and their uses — a 400 year history*, 1975.

Journal of Cherokee Studies, Volume IV, Number 2, Spring 1979, quoted from "Cherokee Education," *The New York Spectator*, New York, New York, November 23, 1821.
—————— Volume IV, Number 2, Spring 1979, quoted from "A Visit to New Echota," *The New York American*, New York, New York, July 16, 1838.

Kilpatrick, Jack Frederick and Anna Gritts Kilpatrick, *New Echota Letters, Contributions of Samuel A. Worcester to the Cherokee Phoenix*, Southern Methodist University Press, 1968.

McLoughlin, William G., *Cherokee Renascence in the New Republic*, Princeton University Press, 1986.

Mooney, James, *Myths of the Cherokee*, Bureau of American Ethnology, 1900.

Moulton, Gary E., *John Ross, Cherokee Chief*, Brown Thrasher Books, University of Georgia Press, 1978.

Perdue, Theda, *Slavery and the Evolution of the Cherokee Society 1540-1866*, University of Tennessee Press, copyright 1979.

Wilkins, Thurman, *Cherokee Tragedy, The Story of the Ridge Family and of the Decimation of a People*, The MacMillan Company, New York, 1970.

Selected Reading List

Claro, Nicole, *The Cherokee Indians*, Chelsea House Publishers, New York.

Cwiklik, Robert, *Sequoyah and the Cherokee Alphabet*, Silver Burdett Press, Englewood Cliffs, N.J., 1989.

Hoobler, Dorothy and Thomas, *The Trail On Which They Wept, The Story of a Cherokee Girl*, Silver Burdett Press, Morristown, 1972.

Leftwich, Rodney L., *Arts and Crafts of the Cherokee*, Cherokee Publications, Cherokee, N.C., 1970.

Oppenheim, Joanne, *Sequoyah, Cherokee Hero*, Troll Associates, Mahwah, N.J., 1979.

Stanton-Rich, Diane, *Stories and Art of the Eastern Band of Cherokee*, Historic Press, Gatlinburg, 1993.

About the Author

With a background in library science and social studies education, Madeleine Meyers finds researching specific events in history both fascinating and fun. "As a former school media specialist, I tried to find books with the interesting details of history that will get students involved in the social sciences. Now I have the enjoyment of searching through old newspapers and histories to produce books that I hope will fill the need."

Ms. Meyers first became fascinated with the story of the Cherokees while studying Georgia history during the ten years she and her family lived there. She has visited the Cherokee, North Carolina area several times in order to see the arts and crafts of the Cherokee Indians, and to learn more about their culture. Ms. Meyers now lives in New England with her husband and two sons.

In her free time, she enjoys reading, travelling, gardening, and writing. Ms. Meyers has written a weekly newspaper column on local history, and is presently working on two novels.